THE WOODLANDS ART BENCHES: SPARKING CONNECTIONS

By Dede Fox

Copyright © 2023 Dede Fox

All rights reserved.

No part of this book may be reproduced or used in any manner without the prior written permission of the copyright owner, except for the use of brief quotations in a book review.

To request permissions, contact the publisher at ssermas@typingmonkeypublishers.com.

ISBN 979-8-9876600-0-3 (first printing)

ISBN 979-8-9876600-3-4 (revised, July 2023)

Cover Art by Kimberly Platt

Layout by Stephanie Sermas

Photographs of "Bean," "The Woodlands Wind-O," "On the Bayou," and "Unmasked Symbiosis" by Joan Tilton

All Other Photographs by Dede Fox

Published by

Typing Monkey Publishers, LLC

www,typingmonkeypublishers.com

For Nickole Kerner Bobley,
Creator of ArtFeel

PREFACE

In September of 2019, local arts and culture writer Nickole Kerner Bobley asked me to compose a poem about "Unmasked Symbiosis," a Woodlands art bench by Argentinian-born artist Gaston Carrio. She suggested I read it at ArtFeel, an event initiated by The Woodlands Art Council encouraging residents to engage with public art.

Even though I was anxious about whether a poem would hold the attention of those seated on the lawn of Market Street Square, I was happy to accept the challenge. In outdoor venues, visuals are a must so I kept my poem concise and full of imagery. The art bench reading went well, thanks to Nickole, a masterful producer, who celebrates everyone's artistry by planning diverse performances.

The red lightning of "Unmasked Symbiosis" sparked my first poem. As I sat on it, my fingers smoothed its sun-warmed metal, and I took a deep breath. It came alive to me—its angles, symmetry, clever construction, and bold color. The sculpture rests on the manicured lawn of a high-rise building, its windows mirroring the natural beauty along the shores of the lake, triggering strong memories.

Before the lake existed, more than forty years ago, my family moved to The Woodlands when the population was 12,000. In the mid-eighties, my daughters, their dad, and I played in the mud at "The Bottom of the Lake Festival" before it was filled with water. That celebration included the unveiling of the massive "Rise of the Midgard Serpent," one of the earliest of over a hundred works of well-loved public art. And this one resides in the lake!

So much has changed since then, as my family and our community have grown. Today the scents of grilled meat from Restaurant Row tempt residents and visitors. Opportunities for refreshment, retail, and recreation surround us. With gratitude, I'm still here, now one of 120,000 residents.

When the pandemic shut down our world in 2020, my daily walks and interactions with the art became a connection I needed. Those excursions soon formed a pattern. I'd sit on the benches, sometimes multiple times and gather sensory input. Scribbled notes on scraps of paper grew into a binder full of details as well as the thoughts, feelings, and memories they inspired. I used my iPhone to photograph the art and their nameplates which list title, artist, sponsor, and year of installation. Those observations and photographs became the framework for this book.

Another positive side effect of the Covid isolation is that poets from across the world now offer guidance to each other via Zoom. In virtual writing classes held by Miah Arnold from Grackle and Grackle and David Meischen from Dos Gatos Press, I had many poems workshopped. Some have been read at previous ArtFeel or Writers in the Schools events. Some have been posted in juried ekphrastic poetry anthologies like those created by Matt Riley at the Friendswood Public Library. Eventually this book coalesced into a collection of photos and poems about twenty-four art benches. As Montgomery County Poet Laureate from 2017-2022, I hoped to complete this manuscript by the end of my term. Here it is, not a moment too soon.

Dede Fox
December 31, 2022

You Are Loved, 2020
Artists: Michelle Old, Stacey Moore, Kevin Giuseppetti
Donors: Debbie and Sparky Gullo in memory of Austin Gullo
Location: back of Town Green Park at Waterway

ETERNAL

Loved announces itself
with a pop of neon red,
stars in post-Covid prom pics.
Short-skirted girls in bloom
arrange their shimmer,
take center stage with practiced smiles
next to not-quite-manly dates,
who hope for more than a goodnight kiss,
all things possible at eighteen.

Families pose here too.
Fathers flex muscles
grip periscope-round speakers
or the tall pipes of *l* and *d*.
Children point to swan boats
at Riva Ridge, beg for a ride
while mothers swat down their arms,
ask them to stand up straight and smile.
All settle on the bony pipes
that form o-v-e,
hoping for that perfect photo
of their not-so-perfect families.

Joggers and walkers
pound past, some smile,
discover new thoughts, dreams
to keep them in the zone
as honeymooners from hotels
along the Waterway
pause to whisper secrets
through the speakers.

But after the sun slips away
and silence descends,
a boy's spirit skips
across the metal surface,
crisscrosses the coils,
dangles from the rounded heights,
the art his playground,
a profound reminder
of his parents' infinite love.

Caetano's Peace, 2014
Artist: Rollin Karg
Donors: Benchmark Hospitality International
Location: in Waterway behind Westin

SPIN, BOWLS, SPIN

Behind Westin's delivery dock,
    across the alley from Alex Katz's Flowers,
        nestled among cypresses
            lining the waterway
                near Woodloch Forest bridge,

a magician's trick creates an illusion--
whirling bowls, blown glass,
sapphire with scalloped edges
atop a tripod of silver pipes, graduated
lengths ascending into branches.

Six flowers pinwheel in color:
green one with cobalt center,
undulating waves, orange rim--
its sister with blue and green striations,
rimmed in red that bleeds to green,

two more with nested black ripples.
Reflections from skyscraper windows
distort shapes, mix green to deep purple,
shifting kaleidoscopic, dichroic colors.
Spin, bowls, spin.

A man on the path, smelling of sandalwood soap,
pauses to discuss the art with his companion.
*Like Chihuly's blossoms…Bellagio's
ceiling…Vegas…inspired by Brazilian…
Caetano Veloso's musical compositions.*

I eavesdrop from the polished granite bench,
run fingers over cool flickers of crystal
playing hide-and-seek in dwindling
sunlight. Braced by a pole, I look up
into the swirl of colors and blink.

Mipenipa, 2016
Artist: Chris Miller
Donors: Mitchell, Peggy, Nicholas & Patrick Hausman
Location: between Waterway Square and Waterway

MIPENIPA MYSTERIES

Like the rocks at Stonehenge
the art bench protects secrets
that emerge from the speckled block
of gray and black granite.

Solid and eternal yet whimsical,
even its name Mipenipa is odd,
nowhere to be found in a dictionary
or Google.

Walkers sit here along the muted water,
silent except for the imagined splash
as a turtle rises from the stone form's
partially submerged log.

A fish head with frog legs emerges
from the core. On one side, its faded eye
reads a miniature book
braced by rocky cypress knees.

An unseen hand has chiseled four lily pads
or are they Pac men, and in one corner
of the curiously comfortable bench
are three-toed bird tracks.

Mipenipa hides
its secrets right
out in the open
as we all do.

Mystical Senses, 2020
Artist: Gaston Carrio
Donors: Amy Cope-Gibbs & Jon Gibbs
Location: between Town Green Park and Riva Row Boathouse

MYSTICAL JOURNEY

Passersby pause to observe
the art bench's otherworldly glow.
Overlapping metal scales
cover its elliptical exterior.
Orbit tipped to one side,
it reflects blazing Texas sunlight.

The dark vortex draws me in.
I climb inside,
relish the sun-warmed planks,
varnished and riveted crosswise
along its interior, where I can
draw my feet up and lean back into its curves.
I run fingers over hole-punched steel
sidewalls that create eerie hollow music.

I breathe and reflect on this realm.
Swans with churning human legs
ripple the waterway.
Children wave from balconies
of turreted apartments
while jets trail silver and white
above the Pavilion's triple tents.

Under a tree with twinkling lights,
next to the bulrushes,
my voyage begins.
Cascading water whooshes
through rocks on either side
as I spin into a new dimension,
escape Covid, and find peace.

Photo Credit: Joan Tilton

Bean, 2016
Artist: Valerie Theberge
Donors: Gayle & Todd Kuoni
Location: on library side of Town Green Park by Story Book Maze

ANOTHER PURIM STORY

She sits by the literary labyrinth,
relaxed yet regal on the bean-shaped bench,
its arms, back, and seat rounded
as her lush body.

Queen Esther tells her story,
a Persian fairy tale disguised
as a book of the Bible,
for her daughters…
and Vashti's.

From her emerald green-tiled throne,
bold shapes emerge in oranges, lavender,
yellow. Circles cradle sets of triangles,
rock them in their curves.

Touching sunlit tiles, some inlaid with gold,
Esther scorches tender fingertips,
only then notices a caution sign
that warns of their danger.

Even so, she touches them again,
welcomes the sensation as she continues
the story of two women,
beautiful and strong as this bench.
They spoke up.

Texas Dawn Water Lily Pad, 2020
Artist: Kyle Thornley
Donors: Heather, Shin & Seth Dickens
Location: across Waterway behind Cynthia Woods Mitchell Pavilion

FROG OPERA

From the south side of the Pavilion,
five metallic lily pads cluster
with a sixth one nearby.
Yellow Dazzlers festoon them,
their blossoms held high,
backing the chartreuse green benches.

Banners announce the Woodlands Waterway,
where Crepe Myrtle blossoms float
languidly in the still July heat.
Riders pedal downstream on swan boats,
the silence of a humid Texas day broken
by their rhythmic paddles.

Joggers, children on scooters, travelers
with backpacks brave the steamy paths
where not even birds chirp.
People wait here for the next trolley,
welcome the comfort of a place to sit
in the shade, watch a small girl in a sundress
who empties a bag of crumbs into the water,
not a duck in sight. Then she exits,
making a game of walking backwards
across the brick walkway with her mother.

At nightfall, a hot breeze stirs up.
Swatting away mosquitoes, people leave.
Green tree frogs gather on lily pads.
Their conductor, on a separate one,
brings the male chorus to order, chiding them
for fighting over a dead June bug.
He reminds them, at intermission
there's an all-you-can eat buffet
of flies, ants, crickets, beetles, and moths.

With a flick of his suction-tipped toes,
The maestro leads the orchestra.
B-beeps fill the air, along with trills
and occasional horn-like blasts.
Wrapped around tree trunks, twinkle lights
spotlight the enchanted performers. On stage
for all to hear, the artists are a free warmup act,
before stars rock the Pavilion stage.

Quercus, 2018
Artist: Owen Dixon
Donors: Jeff & Deborah Coburn
Location: Hughes Landing on Restaurant Row

MOURNING SHADOWS

Quercus, art bench camouflaged under leafy oaks, lives up to its genus. Half-hidden among foliage on an esplanade dappled with sunlight, its salvaged steel back, black lace, draws me in, triggers unexpected thoughts of my grandparents. Light flickers from plasma cutouts, forms inky patterns among shrinking morning shadows. Rough edges line the slab seat, and a textured armrest looks like wood, except for tiny pockmarks formed as artist Owen Dixon smoothed the cement. Like long-ago bubbles, shadowy memories of my grandparents rise to the surface, set in time.

After Grandpa's heart attack, they moved to an apartment near Houston's Medical Center and shady Hermann Park. A few years later, he died. The night of his funeral, I lay in his bed next to my sleeping grandmother, listened to the clocks he repaired chime quarter hours, reminder of all the time we would live without him.

But Grandma, all eighty-three pounds, survived five more years. She moved in clouds of baby powder and White Shoulders, smoothed soft skin with Ponds cold cream. Under starched dresses she hid silky stockings and lacy white slips, created an appearance that belied the dark woods of her life.

After eighth grade, Grandma left school to work. Matched in marriage, she waited on Grandpa's customers while raising three children. Sons, soon six feet tall, towered over her 4'10" frame. All, even her daughter, my mother, earned degrees from Rice and Penn State.

Delicate and strong. Quercus. A tree of life with thirteen grandchildren. Today the rising sun exposes her mysterious shadows, shapes that don't play, positions forever fixed.

Stardust, 2016
Artist: Elizabeth Akamatsu
Donors: Dr. David & Brenda Gottlieb
Location: across Waterway between Town Green Park and Pavilion

STARDUST DAYS

Framed by feathery cypress trees
the metal-red Stardust bench
welcomes strollers
along a curve in the waterway
where the breeze ripples water
and lifts hair.

Snowflake shaped pieces,
like magnetic two-dimensional toys,
fit together, support the structure.
An upright disk, as ornate as *papel picado*,
divides the bench, provides seating on both sides.

Children flock,
climb onto the lower shelf.
Papas and Mamas rest on the higher one,
watch the swan boats nearby
nestle nose to nose,
awaiting their next riders.

Little ones find handholds
and magic in the peek-a-boo cutouts,
curved shapes with unbroken lines:
petals, butterflies, cookies,
airplanes, balloons, smiles—
a place to pretend, to tell stories.

Sticky-warm little fingers
poke through openings,
touch Mamas and Papas,
while cicadas hum and
the nearby falls murmur.
We are all made of Stardust.

Ode to Joy, 2014
Artist: Dan Skaggs
Donors: The Cynthia Woods Mitchell Pavilion
Location: southside steps behind The Cynthia Woods Mitchell Pavilion

BY THE SOUTH GATE

Lights line a pebble stone staircase, exit
for concert goers after Pavilion performances.
Walkways lead down,
    down,
       down
          to Ode to Joy.

Recently trimmed grass scatters across the seat, a curvilinear, Carrara-marble keyboard with flats and sharps slightly raised in black granite. Off-white tiles line the façade. Cracked keys and well-worn, patched edges reflect its use.

Hopeful half and quarter notes rise from a musical staff fashioned as a stainless-steel backrest. Bars and lines angle, press like impatient fingers urging those seated to rise and rejoice. Strong, simple melodies meld with imagination.

In 1785, German poet Friedrich Schiller created the lyrics. Beethoven put the praise poem to music with wishes for peace and freedom among all people. Today walkers march out with joy. As the translated lyrics sing,

The magic binds again
What custom strictly divided
All people become brothers,
Where the gentle wing abides.

Family Tree, 2016
Artist: Don Lawler
Donors: Highland Woods Health
Location: between Six Pines Dr. and Waterway Avenue along Waterway

ABIDING BEAUTY

Sculptor Don Lawler began
with a 9000-pound limestone block
composed of shell fragments and tiny fossils--
now solid, exquisite, enduring--
the oldest rock found throughout the world.

Using a diamond blade on a grinder
the artist inscribed design lines first,
then drilled holes for feathers and wedges.
He hammered to increase pressure
and break away surplus sections.
Holes for stainless steel pins and epoxy
were predrilled at the base for installation later.
On the Restless Rock Blog, the artist recorded
the intense process and heavy lifting.
A 23-ton crane hauled it to the artist's workshop
in its 7,800-pound form. Family Tree's
creation required vision and planning.

To make room for the curved bench,
Lawler removed a large volume of stone.
He flipped a 1000-pound piece to the ground
with a metal pry bar before rolling the larger
chunk into the studio on a rail cart.
With slow refining and finishing,
he fashioned symmetrical trunks and
finger-like branches for beauty and support.
To bring life to the sculpture, the artist
chiseled texture into a multitude
of heart-shaped leaves, layered like passing years.
Creation requires skill and determination.

A crane returned to load the 4,000-pound sculpture
onto a Thrifty flatbed for the 900 miles trip
from Kentucky to its new Texas home.
Later the Heave Ho Crane Company
lifted it onto its concrete pad, in an alcove
behind the Woodlands Waterway Marriott.
Today couples sit on the bench's smooth,
strong curve, no armrests to separate them.
Love and patience create family.

Penstemon, 2020
Artist: Daniel Hornung
Donors: Beth & Doug Grijalva
Location: behind South County Libary along Waterway

IMMUTABLE PROMISE

Fuschia flowers with yellow centers
Tip their faces to the sun.
Blossoms cap a single four-sided metal stalk,
towering high above two symmetrical benches
shaped like green leaves,
veined with slits for air flow.
Gnats race across unbroken surfaces
in circular patterns while pine needles
nestle in crevices formed by bolted metal.
Also known as Beardtongue,
a favorite of hummingbirds,
a penstemon favors hot, sunny days.

Up to six people fit on the seats,
three on either side, where they can admire
the action on the waterway below.
A bare-chested kayaker paddles.
He has shaved both sides of his head,
but his mohawk sports a long, black tail.
A cigarette dangles from his mouth
as he crosses paths with a couple in life jackets,
rowing in tandem. All of this is tucked away,
hidden behind a library whose commissioner
wears blinders, cuts book budgets while demanding
his own parking space in the crowded lot.

At sunset, rays of light break
through darkening clouds, reflect
off the roof of a trolley stop.
Benches extend leaf arms,
outstretched like a yoga pose,
palms up, embracing the sky.
At the top of the tapered stem,
proud and strong buds,
survivors of the sculpture's
installation during a pandemic,
promise hope, renewed life, unimpeded
growth, a perennial "Penstemon."

Photo Credit: Joan Tilton

Unmasked Symbiosis, 2018
Artist: Gaston Carrio
Donors: Strike
Location: Hughes Landing behind Restaurant Row by office building

STRONGER TOGETHER

A deception of movement
in twin flashes of Radio Flyer red
steel welded together,
secured to pebbled concrete.
Shadows disguise undersides,
the illusion of black streaks
when only a few upright posts
bear that absence of color.

Skeletal handprints
and feather gray footprints
of sneakered children
in alligator patterned soles
climb sloped zigzags
to a solid center,
a sun-warmed bench
at the axes of its wings.

Light Balls, 2014
Artist: Manfred Kielnhofer
Donors: The Howard Hughes Corporation®
Location: Waterway Square

WHEN SUMMER HEAT BREAKS

People flock to Waterway Square,
a *zocalo* where all gather
to enjoy the final September sunset.
Twinkle lights spiral every trunk
and the lower branches of trees.
They illuminate walkways lined with benches.

Three white orbs support
a modified T-shaped bench,
with a shortened crosspiece on one side,
its seating planks of espresso-stained wood.
One on each end, round cut-outs, expose
the tops of three globes,

where little ones with high-pitched voices
scramble up and dance to distant salsa drum beats.
They squeal and giggle as the bench shakes.
One rolls his Hot Wheels over a sphere
as another does cartwheels on the lawn.
A small girl with a big bow and glitter pink shoes
twirls and extends a hand to her father.

There's a constant murmur of water
as it rushes over the block-long bricked wall.
Fifteen gushers shoot upward, their changing colors
reminiscent of neon fountains in Las Vegas—
electric blues, limes and oranges dance with magenta.

Aromas of grilled steak, onions, peppers and hot oil
fill the air as young couples in designer labels stroll,
with frequent pauses for selfies as they wait
for tables to open up. A pregnant woman leads a man
in a KN95 mask from Cyclone Anaya's, as another
with purple hair and a long Boho dress enters.

Older tourists in sunhats and shorts pause
to survey the scene while two Latino families
play with toddler sons, proudly dressed
for Friday night in ironed shorts and tops.
Sweethearts line the balcony at street level
to sneak kisses under a sliver of fall moon.

Resolute, 2018
Artist: Paul Reimer
Donors: The Dorman Family in Memory of Matt Dorman
Location: by Lakes Edge Boathouse in Hughes Landing

A white-haired man sits alone on the Light Ball Bench,
fading like the sunlight while he counts the years,
remembers date nights like those he's witnessing.
As if a fairy godmother answers his wish,
the light balls awaken, illuminate a synchronized
ballet of green to blue to pink and back again.
Onlookers ooh and ahh. Even the old man glows.

RESILIENT

Bare metal branches sway to one side
as if windblown, determined to survive.
Limbs graceful as dancers' arms
point to a cypress at Lakes Edge
Boathouse, where a dozen ducks
doze or peck at feathers in shade,
tucked away behind midrise apartments
                            at Hughes Landing.

Claw-like roots anchor the iron tree
along one side of a stone bench,
leaving room for people to sit
on the warm flat stone, striated
in shades of ochre, rust, gray, and white,
a place to reflect on facing adversity.
Like the Great Blue Herons that skim
the lake's surface seeking sustenance,
                            they will rise again.

Family, 2014
Artist: Terrell Powell
Donors: Gordy & Michelle Bunch
Location: Woodlands Mall facing Waterway

BIRDSONG

Charming as Mo Willems's pigeons,
primitive birds, button-eyed and watchful,
stand sentry behind a crayon blue bench
with cozy rounded armrests
warmed by the sun.

Mustard and terra cotta-colored vines
twist across the bench's façade,
as if the quirky birds, brilliant in primary colors
roost on the branch of a whimsical tree
Without ears, these birds hear nothing, see all.

The shortest fowl reaches upward
touches his beak to another's, perhaps
waiting to be fed by his mother.
She and the tiniest one face each other,
but their round eyes watch others watch them.

All five have white dots on their irises
that form dots within dots
within dots within dots of bold color.
Swirls of paint in unbroken circles
create their heads and bodies.

None have wings or legs,
except for the two guards
outside the bench's armrests.
Those birds have stick thin legs in striped socks
like the silenced witches in the Wizard of Oz.

Beaks painted shut,
the birds are silent.
No warbles, tweets, stirring trills.
Oh, the secrets they could tell
about what they see. But can't.

Crete Bench Rest, 2014
Artist: Victoria Goldstein
Donors: The Woodlands Art Council
Location: between Waterway Square and Waterway Square Bridge by Waterway

DREAMING FOR ONE, PLEASE

From the far side of the water,
It looks like a wave runner,
Or a compact boat, narrow nose
ready to slice through surf.

To walkers on the waterway path
it first resembles a curved couch,
at once sleek and plush,
a contemporary loveseat.

Up close it's more like the stark
white rocks, walkways, and buildings
pictured in posters of Crete, sandwiched
between Aegean and Mediterranean Seas.

Curved like a dolphin, the Crete Bench
swims through cerulean oceans.
Water collects in a dip on its tail,
its seating surface rounded and slippery.

Only one can sit comfortably,
eyes closed in the sunlight.
A bench, a boat, a dolphin?
Here is a place to dream alone.

Why Sit When You Can Play? 2018
Artist: The Urban Conga
Donors: The Alex & Sharon Sutton Family
Location: between Waterway Avenue and Waterway Square by Waterway

ANTI-BENCH

Like a toy from the Neiman Marcus
online Fantasy Gift catalog,
this oversized xylophone invites all
to pick up metal rods and make music.

Shaped like a wave suggesting perpetual
motion, it asks, "Why Sit When You Can Play?"
The toy-blue metal frame resembles a desktop
file sorter with accordion-pleated slats,
braced by rods, capable of storing musical notes.
But inside, an open space runs the length
of the instrument through the core,
narrowing to a trapezoidal space at one end.

Inset at the top of the bench, colored bars
shaped like rectangular prisms,
provide the only place to sit,
cold on a cloudy morning,
yet they beg to be played.
Batons, attached to the bench
by twisted steel wires covered in plastic,
invite everyone to stop and play awhile.

Musicians of all sizes hit the keys,
match the thump of feet
as runners jog along the walkways
that line the river and inhale meaty
aromas from a Mexican kitchen.
There's a soft rush of cars passing
over the Waterway Avenue bridge,
as fall leaves float on the surface of the water.

The anti-bench dares walkers to sit, even
provides a curve on either side to tuck feet,
but the cold keys press against bottoms,
urging all to get up,
make music,
with notes in bold colors:
blue, green, yellow, and pink.
No full scales but plenty of music possible.

Photo Credit: Joan Tilton

The Woodlands Wind-O, 2018
Artist: STEREOTANK
Donors: Michael & Vicki Richmond
Location: at end of Restaurant Row between restaurants and Lake Woodlands

WIND-O REVERSO

At the end of Restaurant Row
sits an empty frame of yellow metal
angled adjacent to the still water
where this art bench has two views,
a reminder this is an oasis.
Quacking ducks pop up and down,
searching for an aquatic dinner.
Over a blue-sky lake, herons fly low,
the centerpiece of the flat landscape.
Hidden from the other side, no one can see
immigrants work behind tinted glass,
prepare shrimp and snapper for the fortunate.

Prepare shrimp and snapper for the fortunate.
Immigrants work behind tinted glass,
hidden from the other side. No one can see
the centerpiece of the flat landscape.
Over a blue sky-lake, herons fly low,
searching for an aquatic dinner,
Quacking ducks pop up and down,
a reminder this is an oasis.
Where this art bench has two views,
angled adjacent to the still water,
sits an empty frame of yellow metal
at the end of Restaurant Row.

Foot Rest, 2014
Artist: Rod Flower
Donors: Dr. Robert & Renee Neville
Location: behind Woodlands Mall by restaurants along Waterway

FOOTSIES

Four outward-facing man-sized feet
attached to strong ankles and solid calves
support the mustard yellow Foot Rest
bench created with 3D foam and paint.
Scratches, cracks, and dents mar
a few bare toes, a reminder of the art
sponsors, a clever podiatrist and his family.

Eight feet emerge in relief from the high,
hard back. At the top, toes play footsies
as they overlap in sets of two—blue and burnt orange,
purple and turquoise. Beneath them,
four raised, side-by side feet are evenly spaced—
crimson and green, teal and magenta. Like a Thai
massage, toes press into the backs of those seated.

Resembling an amusement park ride
in Disney bold colors, the bench beckons
to people wanting to take a load off,
perhaps after walking the mall for hours.
The exhausted drop, hope for
an invisible seat belt to secure imaginations
before take-off, a fanciful tour with aerial
views of the Waterway, Pavilion, Market Street,
Hughes Landing, Lake Woodlands, and beyond.

Reality lands riders back where they started,
waiting for a table across from entrances
to popular restaurants. By now, many
have found their feet and are ready to eat.

Amber, 2014
Artist: Luis Pavón
Donors: The Woodforest National Bank
Location: at base of Town Green Park facing Waterway

CAPTIVE

Like fern fronds embedded
in the bench's amber back support,
the man doesn't move.

He has his back to the statue of George Mitchell,
founder of The Woodlands, as the developer
raises his sculpted right hand in blessing.

Behind his oversized sunglasses, the seated
man's bronze face betrays nothing. Wearing
a non-descript cap, he hides his age.

Dressed in black--t-shirt, shorts,
and running shoes--he leaves his phone
at his side, a bottle of water at his feet.

Motionless, he faces the canal,
leaving little emotional space for others
on the live-edge wooden bench.

Shades of ochre run through the plank,
where unseen hands have picked at the finish,
exposing the grain in places, occasional gouges.

Immobile for long periods of time--
thirty minutes, an hour--
the man claims this shady spot in Town Green.

Others in the park may not know
Sunday is the longest day
for one who lives alone.

Photo Credit: Joan Tilton

On the Bayou, 2016
Artist: John V. Weber
Donors: Peggy & Ray Wilcox
Location: at Riva Row Boat House facing turning basin

BAYOU HOME

By the silent bayou,
a triumphant bird clasps
a silver-scaled fish in its pointed beak,
perches on a stainless-steel stump
with visible striations, washboard ridges,
an artist's interpretation of the trunk
of a bald cypress, bark stripped away
on one side. John V. Webber's hollow
sculpture glints in the sunlight
under a winter blue sky.

A wooden bench, sun warmed
and sanded smooth, encircles the tree,
provides outward-looking seats for six
above a round concrete platform.
In the air, fragrant notes of Sweetspire
and Zydeco intertwine. Unflappable,
the forward-facing bird can't see
her tail feathers, tarnished by moisture,
heat, and chemicals, nor wonder how
what's behind affects what lies ahead.

Umbrella Tree, 2016
Artist: Dan Skaggs
Donors: The Shedden Family
Location: Riva Row behind Boat House

LIKE THE EGRETS

From a distance
it looks like a bird flying
low between the oaks
after dipping for fish in the channel
by Riva Row Boat House.

Closer, up the hill above the docks,
it looks like a bouquet, four welded pipes
gathered together, topped with metal leaves.
They overlap, as autumn leaves might
when they fall on a windy day.

Water rings the round base,
like soiled liquid from an overturned planter,
and cracks in the low bench's beige grout
confirm this umbrella offers no protection
from foul weather.

Woodlands' trees dwarf this manmade one,
enclosed within a semicircular stone wall,
comfortable height for adult seating
while the lower bench encircles the tree,
perfect gathering spot for children.

Families congregate here, meet friends.
Paths and parks, a waterway with boats
and art spread out before them.
They plan excursions or simply look up.
Adults journey back to childhood,

remember lying on the grass under branches,
peeking through leaves as the shape-sifting
clouds race into the unknown, a reminder
that someday they and their offspring,
like the egrets, will fly away too.

Hail and Farewell, Henry Moore
Artist: Bob Mosier
Donors: Rob & Cindy Hardin
Location: currently not available

HAUL AND FAREWELL

Where is the playful tiered sculpture
built from African Mahogany,
the one with four built-in benches,
four unique views?

Time after time, map in hand,
I find nothing but an empty
cement pad stripped bare,
not even an identifying plaque.

When I meet a park ranger, I ask
if the art bench is a victim of extreme
Texas weather. All he knows--
someone hauled it away.

Come back, Henry Moore. Come back.

Proud Souls, 2018
Artist: Gaston Carrio
Donors: Memorial Hermann The Woodlands Medical Center
Location: between Town Green Park and South County Library on Waterway

VARIATIONS ON *PROUD SOULS*

I

Upright, like open hands,
curved and raised in blessing,
never again to touch the other,
curved metal pipes quiver.
As two souls reach for heaven,
the wooden bench connects them,
a reminder of their union,
earthbound, two becoming one,
generations created, a multitude.
Victorious, the souls rise.

II

No one sits on my bench when it rains.
Drizzle beads my curved vertical strands.
Teardrops grow heavy and trickle
Down my metal filaments.
Showers wash me clean.

No one hears my music when it rains,
But during storms, you can feel the thunder
In my pipes, vibrations as winds play
The strings of my dual harps.

III

If a girl shares the same line
of latitude with the sculpture
and observes its structure from either side,
she'll see enormous open fans
their bases grounded on a grassy lawn,
its arc straining to touch spring green
needles in a nearby patch of tall pines.
Dreams whisper through the fan's frame,
while she listens from a distance.

IV

Hashkiveinu
"Shelter us beneath your wings,"
Debbie Friedman sings a prayer
for us to lie down in peace at night
and to return to life the next day.
Her angelic voice rises in our memories
long after her death.

Between wings, mirror images,
we listen from the bench.
Lyrics and musical notes
enfold us, feathered
with promises of light and love

V

Two proud souls ascend.
The Eternal Mother rocks
them in heaven's arms.

NOTES

If you woud like to visit these (and other) art benches, please visit the link below for a map to help you plan your journey.

https://www.thewoodlandsartscouncil.org/p/programs/public-art/art-bench-project1

Dede Fox was the 2016-2019 NEA Writer at Bryan Federal Prison Camp for Women and the 2017-2022 Montgomery County Poet Laureate. Through Writers in the Schools and the Periwinkle Foundation, she continues to write with hematology/oncology patients at Texas Children's Hospital.

Her publications include *The Treasure in the Tiny Blue Tin* (TCU Press), and *On Wings of Silence: Mexico '68* (Lamar University Literary Press), a novel in verse. Other works are the poetry books *Postcards Home (*Ink Brush Press*)* and *Confessions of a Jewish Texan (*Poetica Press), as well as nonfiction for *Highlights Magazine*. Dede's book reviews and poetry have appeared in multiple journals and blogs.

When she's not reading, writing, or walking wooded trails, Dede loves hanging out with her daughters, their spouses, four grandchildren, and her devoted dogs Cinnamon and Sugar.

www.ingramcontent.com/pod-product-compliance
Lightning Source LLC
Chambersburg PA
CBHW042055060526
44119CB00118B/324